Margaret Roberts

◆ LITTLE BOOK OF ◆

MINT

ISBN 1 86812 674 9

First edition, first impression 1997

Published by Southern Book Publishers (Pty) Ltd
PO Box 3103, Halfway House, 1685

Design and DTP by Tracey Mackenzie
Set in 10 on 12 point Palatino
Cover photograph by Cath Simpson
Illustrations by Margaret Roberts
Printed and bound by National Book Printers,
Drukkery Street, Goodwood, Western Cape

Contents

Origins

Through the centuries mint has been a much loved herb, revered for its remarkable fragrant, medicinal, culinary and cosmetic properties.

The Ebers papyrus, dating from around 1550 BC and probably one of the oldest recorded medical texts, recorded mint — particularly peppermint — as an effective treatment for indigestion. Herbalists in the Middle Ages, too, recorded the use of mint tea to aid digestion, ease abdominal bloating and stomach ache, to assist childbirth and as an antidote for the bites of scorpions and mad dogs!

Mint was used as a breath freshener, particularly to mask the odours of alcohol, and bunches of fresh mint were carried in pouches to the eating houses to mask the tell-tale signs of over-indulgence. Pomanders of crushed mint were worn to mask the putrid odours of open sewers, and mint was probably one of the earliest herbs to feature in tussie-mussies, those delightful little posies of fragrant herbs and flowers kept at hand to repel odours and germs and keep illness at bay.

The ancient Hebrews used mint on the floors of the synagogues to be crushed underfoot to freshen the air and revive and rejuvenate tired pilgrims.

In ancient Greece bunches of mint were tied together and floated in the water amongst the bathers in public bath houses, to freshen and sanitise the water. Very early paintings from both Greece and Egypt depict mint as a herb with which the dead were buried, poultices were bound, as a beauty treatment, and as an ingredient in both food and wine.

In Roman mythology the beautiful nymph Minthe was Pluto's lover. On discovering them together Pluto's enraged wife, Prosperine, turned Minthe into a plant that would have in its fragrance 'the ardour of love as well as the scent of fear'. The legend goes that Minthe's fragrance was so haunting and so lingered in his senses, that he never forgot her!

Mint is native to the Middle East, but by the end of the ninth century many varieties of mint had been introduced to Europe, where it became a symbol of hospitality and friendship. Over the centuries its medicinal and fragrant properties have made it one of the world's most popular herbs, and it has an important place in both traditional and alternative medicine, cosmetics and cooking, as well as folk lore.

The Romans were reputedly the first to experiment with mint in cooking, and then mint was used, as it is today, to flavour sauces, meats, wines and other drinks with its sublime, refreshing taste.

There are estimated to be over 630 varieties of mint in the world today belonging to the genus *Mentha*, part of the great family Labiatae. Like the other members of this family, such as thyme, rosemary, basil, sage and winter savory, mint is a great cross-pollinator and there is enormous confusion, even amongst botanists, as to the names of all the different subspecies and varieties.

Growing mint

All the mints are perennials and love rich, well-composted, moist soil. They eagerly seek out new ground by means of long runners, so edge the beds in which you wish to plant mint with heavy duty plastic, or plant it in large tubs if you want to curb its invasive habits. Well-established clumps of mint will often appear to die off, then send up runners in all directions which, as they settle, send up bright little tufts of succulent, scented leaves, which establish themselves into new clumps.

So many of us remember our grandmothers planting mint under a dripping tap, where it grew prolifically and conveniently for mint sauce all year through. A moist position is perfect for mint and the damp earth and extra nourishment of a spadeful or two of compost every now and then are all that is needed to ensure continuous, healthy growth.

Mint will tolerate a fair amount of shade, although it will struggle in heavy shade. It is one of the few herbs that will thrive in both sun and light or medium shade. I tuck it in all over the garden in a variety of positions and have found it so easy to grow. Should you find that it looks drab or tired, dig it up and transplant it with a few spadefuls of rich compost to a different position, preferably with some sun, or simply try nourishing it with compost and good, regular watering.

Propagate mint by runners or cut off a section with a spade and replant it in well-dug, newly composted ground. Plant the new plants approximately 30 cm apart and, if you wish, edge the beds with heavy plastic strips or plant the mint in big tubs as mentioned earlier to prevent it from spreading uncontrollably.

By removing the flowering heads of mint you will be able to control cross-pollination and keep your species pure. I once grew a mint garden on my farm below a furrow from which the mint beds could be flooded twice weekly. I planted about 20 varieties of mint, including several indigenous varieties, and for a time it was a paradise. I labelled each mint with its correct name, and the place and date it originated. Very efficiently, I made charts and notes on the uses, flavours and conspicuous characteristics of each variety.

As time passed, so my twice yearly composting became less regular and I became too busy to cut off the flowering stems. I ended up with about 40 different mints that no one could identify, all growing profusely! I clearly remember the summer afternoons that botanists stood knee deep in the wonderful aroma of mint, sniffing, examining and exclaiming — or cursing — in utter confusion! I had created, in my ignorance, a 'hornet's nest of mints' as one expert labelled it: the first of its kind in Africa, to their knowledge, on such a scale. Without knowing it I had propagated a whole host of new varieties! We did our best to label and catalogue the new varieties and I then set about stabilising them.

To this day I am always slightly anxious when presented with a mint to identify and will forever wonder if its grandparents came from my beautiful tree-fringed mint garden in the valley at the foot of the great Magaliesberg, many years ago!

Varieties

ৡ

The mints described here are the most popular and readily available species in South Africa, which are well established as specific cultivars. From these major varieties others will have hybridised, which would only be confusing to describe. So, as an elderly botanist has suggested, 'Go by your nose!' If you like its scent, grow it and use it in your own recipes.

Should you stumble upon a new variety, it would be best to plant it as far away as possible from any other mints you have already established in your garden. Remember to cut off the flowering heads in midsummer, to prevent cross-pollination.

GARDEN MINT *Mentha spicata* (also known as *M. viridis*)

This mint is often called **spearmint**, which is surprising when one considers that there are many mints far more reminiscent of spearmint in scent and flavour. This is the commonest of all varieties — the 'lamb-and-mint-sauce' garden mint.

The bright green glossy leaves of this mint are deeply veined and toothed. It is often susceptible to rust and winter die-back and does need to be cut and tidied through summer or it becomes very straggly. My grandmother had this variety growing under her dripping tap and to this day I cannot cook peas without a sprig of garden mint in the water, or eat lamb without that most delectable of condiments, mint sauce, made with this mint.

Garden mint is one of the most voracious seekers of new ground and nourishment, so compost twice yearly, and line the area in which you plant it with plastic if you do not want it to spread uncontrollably.

Garden mint

Apple mint *Mentha sauveolens*

Also called **Bowles mint**, this is another common South African mint, which is perhaps my favourite variety. It almost surpasses garden mint in flavour, is far more stable, it doesn't die back in winter, it is resilient to attacks of rust, and it is a wonderfully vigorous grower.

It is a fairly tall-growing variety, and in good soil can reach up to 1 m in height. Its leaves are large, downy and grey-green, with mauve flowering spikes often branched in threes.

M. villosa var. *alupecuroides* is another variety of apple mint, with smaller leaves. Both varieties are called 'dry land mints' as they tolerate full sun and heat. Although I am seldom in favour of drying herbs, as the flavour of fresh herbs is far superior, this mint is the best for drying as it retains its flavour well.

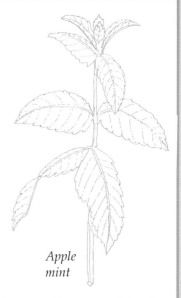

Apple mint

Pineapple mint *Mentha sauveolens variegata*

Sometimes called **variegated apple mint**, this very pretty mint has pale green leaves edged unevenly in palest cream. It is tough and resilient to cold and heat, drought and floods and is one of the few mints that has remained true to form without cross pollination. It is low growing and it can be kept neatly clipped.

Its fresh pineapple fragrance, from which it gets its name, makes it a particularly useful mint for posies and cosmetics.

BLACK PEPPERMINT *Mentha piperita nigra*

This variety of mint is so erratic in its growth habits, it is perhaps best not to have it in too prominent a position! From having great swathes of it one minute, it will seem to all but disappear the next, as its dark purple stems lie horizontally and easily disappear amongst other plants.

New colonies of peppermint can be propagated by forking out a few underground root clusters, called 'stolons', pushing them

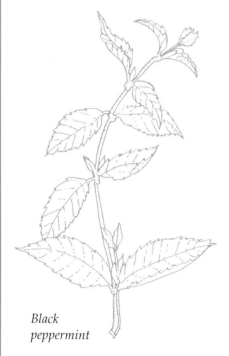

Black peppermint

into moist ground and pressing down well. In very favourable circumstances it will reach 30–40 cm in height, but its growth habit is typically creeping and sprawling and its unobtrusive, small leaves and occasional tiny pale mauve flowers all around the stem are liable to disappear into the undergrowth.

It is intensely fragrant, and can completely overpower all other scents. This is the variety that students seek out for its marvellous brain-stimulating properties — but remember, too much is not a good thing. This is a powerful herb and must be used with discretion.

GREEN PEPPERMINT *Mentha piperita*

Green peppermint — or as I call it, **Greek peppermint** — is far more stable and attractive than its black brother, *M. p. nigra*. It has big, green, fairly smooth leaves and an upright growth habit, making it an excellent pot plant or border. I got mine originally from Greece, a thumb-length sprig that grew so profusely I supplied several nurseries with it in the early 1980s.

The leaves make a refreshing tea after a heavy meal and the whorls of mauve flowers are lovely in salads and desserts. The Greeks use them stir fried in olive oil with onions and aubergines.

EAU DE COLOGNE MINT *Mentha piperita* var. *citrata*

This handsome, rather delicate plant smells exactly like eau de cologne. The stems are ruby red or dark green and the leaves are longish and rounder than most other mints, but like the other mints, there is variation in both colour and shape. Some sprigs reach a height of 30 cm, but mostly they sprawl and disappear amongst other plants.

Flowers appear in clusters, either pink or light mauve, and both the leaves and flowers are lovely added to pot pourris. I find it a temperamental mint to grow, but grow it primarily for its wonderful scent.

Eau de cologne mint

CHOCOLATE MINT *Mentha spicata* var. *piperita*

The origins of this mint are anyone's guess, but its ancestors definitely have peppermint and garden mint in their genealogy. The chocolate overtones are astonishing and chopped into a chocolate cake icing or over chocolate mousse, it is exquisite. One of the African gardeners at the Herbal Centre so aptly described it after a day of planting out new roots as 'iPeppermint Crisp!'

Chocolate mint has pale grey-green leaves on 30–50 cm stems and masses of white or light lilac flowers that attract masses of butterflies. It is perhaps one of the neatest, showiest mints and as it hardly dies down in winter at all, it is attractive all year round. Tidying and pruning back will ensure new growth and keep the plant looking good all year round.

Chocolate mint

This variety is tougher than most others, and must be set apart to prevent cross-pollination, either in separate beds or in large tubs kept handy for picking all year round. Here at the Herbal Centre cross-pollination of chocolate mint with water mint has resulted in a rampant, long-leafed, metre-high hybrid that tastes neither of spearmint nor chocolate! It is nevertheless beautifully revitalising and refreshing in a warm bath or cool drink.

The Italian origins of this mint make it well suited to the heat and dryness of southern Africa.

CAPE VELVET MINT Possibly *Mentha longifolia* var. *wissi*

A botanist friend of mine found this woolly, long-leafed mint along a shady river bank near Meiringspoort in the Cape some years ago, and brought it to the Herbal Centre. It never turned a hair, but just kept on growing! I named it Cape velvet mint owing to its origins and its velvety leaves, and this seems to have been accepted as a common name in horticultural circles.

Unlike any other mint, it forms clumps from which long stalks emerge. These are thick with dark, dull green, velvety leaves and short branchlets on which many clusters of coarse, grey-white flowers form.

The long flowering stems placed in a vase will keep a room fragrant for days and, incidentally, free of both flies and mosquitoes! A velvety leaf in a cup of black coffee after dinner is superb, as the minty taste enhances the taste of the coffee superbly.

This rare and wonderful mint is so easy to grow and I have a big pot of it near the kitchen door for quick pickings. The clump merely gets bigger as it ages and every autumn the long stems should be cut off at the base. The new jewel-like leaves form a round little hump during winter, from which tall flowering stems are sent out in late spring. Its neat form and long flowering period make it a popular mint for the garden.

Cape velvet mint

CORN MINT *Mentha arvensis* (also called *M. aquatica citrata*)

The species name *arvensis* means 'of the fields', and this little mint often grows wild along the field perimeters in Europe. It has smallish, bright green, sharply pointed leaves which are superb in fruit drinks, and for this purpose I grow it prolifically.

It is a low-growing variety, seldom reaching a height of more than 20–25 cm. It spreads easily and persistently by its abundant root system. It hardly ever flowers, which is the main reason that this species has not cross-pollinated and has stayed true to type for all the years that I have been growing it at the Herbal Centre.

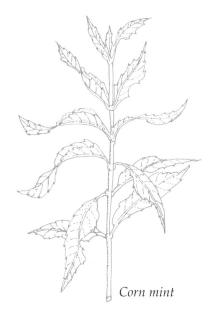

Corn mint

Corn mint is probably the most rewarding of the mints to grow. It is so prolific that it actually benefits from constant clipping back, sending up new uniform sprigs throughout the growing season.

Its wonderfully fresh flavour has made it an exceptionally popular variety of mint in my nursery and indeed all over South Africa.

> ❧ HANDY HINT
> Chew a mint leaf or sip a cup of mint tea to ease indigestion, flatulence and colic.

INDIGENOUS SPEARMINT *Mentha longifolia polyadena*

The fragrance and flavour of this tall, graceful species are truly spearmint. It is the tallest of all the mints, growing easily over 1 m high. It is an extremely vigorous grower and once it is established in your garden you will find it coming up all over the place.

It is found all over South Africa along moist furrows, at the edges of dams and on riverbanks and vleis. The light lime-green leaves are about 10 cm long, narrow and pointed, and are almost hairless. The flowers are white or pale mauvy pink and appear in tall spikes that seem to persist all through summer and into winter. The long sprays need to be cut back severely in winter to make way for new growth in spring.

This species transplants easily with a mere slip of root, and although it is such a prolific grower and tends to become rather untidy, it is easily controlled.

Indigenous spearmint is a tremendous asset in the cook's garden with its wonderfully fresh taste and is particularly delicious chopped on fruit salads and in fruit drinks.

Indigenous spearmint

CAPE SPEARMINT *Mentha longifolia capensis*

Also called **balderjan**, this long-leafed mint has grey-green leaves that are hairier and not quite as long and narrow as those of the indigenous spearmint, but with a similar flavour, which sometimes gives rise to confusion between the two species. This species is found mainly in the Cape, however, and is not quite as robust or as untidy as the indigenous variety. It too has pale white or mauve flowers on long spikes.

Cape spearmint has a respected place in folk medicine, particularly in the Cape, and many recipes still in use today combine it with other ingredients such as cloves, coriander and anise.

Both Cape spearmint and indigenous spearmint are subspecies of European horsemint, *M. longifolia*, which is a smaller variety with similarly long, narrow leaves, but is not nearly as delicious. Both are used medicinally to treat colds, stomach cramp, flatulence and indigestion, and as a poultice to ease muscular aches, pains and swellings.

It propagates easily by rooted stems, and flourishes in moist soil and light shade.

Cape spearmint

WILD WATER MINT *Mentha aquatica*

This is the commonest of the indigenous mints, and may be found growing around dams, vleis and on riverbanks all over South Africa. It is low-growing and creeping, never reaching more than about 30 cm in height. The wide, almost egg-shaped leaves are dull green and sometimes hairy. The flowers occur in small heads of white or palest pink.

The flavour of wild water mint is very strong, and consequently it is used more often medicinally as a tea than for culinary purposes. There are, however, a few delicious traditional recipes that make use of its fresh taste, such as pickled fish and bobotie.

Bunches of this little mint inside a facecloth make a wonderfully refreshing scrub for tired muscles, as many hikers will know.

Wild water mint is easily propagated by merely pulling up a creeping stem with roots all along the nodes, and pressing it into moist soil. It is tough and resilient to disease and the changing seasons, providing its roots are kept constantly moist.

Wild water mint

CORSICAN MINT *Mentha requienii*

Also known as **jewel mint**, this low, bright green, tiny-leafed mint is much sought after for planting between paving stones or edgings. When walked on it releases a strong peppermint fragrance. Only about 2 cm in height, it is compact and neat and very dense, forming a wonderful groundcover under roses or fruit trees, where it is also useful for keeping pests away.

Corsican mint

This is not an edible mint as the others are, but is used rather for its insect-repelling properties. When rubbed to release the oils this little mint, like pennyroyal, will keep mosquitoes at bay. Plant it in wide shallow pots and place it near garden benches where it is lovely to run one's hands over it, thus releasing the insect-repelling oils.

Transplanting is very simple. Merely chop off a portion with a spade and replant the tuft in rich, well-composted soil and keep moist until it establishes itself by sending out little runners.

Like most of the other mints, Corsican mint prefers partial shade but I have also grown it successfully between hot paving stones on a sunny path. Water it more frequently if it grows in a sunny position.

Pennyroyal *Mentha pulegium*

Like Corsican mint, this is a creeping, tiny-leafed mint, which also makes an excellent groundcover. It has a more downy leaf, usually about ½–1 cm in length. The pretty mauve flowers appear in whorls on upright stems above the dense carpet of leaves.

I use this lovely mint in hanging baskets and big shallow tubs, and as a groundcover under tomatoes, strawberries, green peppers, roses and grape vines and it keeps everything insect-free. I plant up large tubs for the patio with it every summer and urge guests to rub their hands over the leaves to release the oils and then to rub their scented hands over their bare legs and arms to keep mosquitoes at bay. Rubbing sprigs over the chair legs will also release the mosquito-repellent oils and ensure a peaceful evening outside.

Pennyroyal

Crushed sprigs pushed down ants' holes keep them away too. My grandmother put bunches of fresh pennyroyal sprigs in her polishing cloths when she dusted the furniture and the whole house was kept fly and ant free with this simple method. In the old days meat was covered in sprigs of pennyroyal to keep it fresh and free of flies.

This little mint is seldom used as a flavouring for food, as it is too strong to take internally but as an insect-repellent it is glorious.

LEMON BALM *Melissa officinalis*

Also called **bee balm**, this wonderful herb is not really a true mint, as it does not have the tendency to spread and seek new ground. But as it is often known as **lemon mint** and, like mint, belongs to the Labiatae family, it surely has a place in this book.

It is a wonderfully easy herb to grow, and will thrive in both full sun and light shade. It grows in a clump of light sprays about 60 cm in height, with scalloped pale green leaves 2–3 cm long. In winter it will die back and needs to be pruned back hard to allow the tender new shoots to appear.

Medicinally lemon balm is a remarkably versatile herb and can be used for ailments as diverse as scorpion stings, nausea, depression and exam nerves. It is one of the most important herbs for soothing, calming and quietening. It is antiviral, antibacterial, antispasmodic and has antioxidant properties!

Divide clumps of lemon balm by chopping off a piece with a spade or pushing two forks back to back to split the clump. Plant the new plants in well-composted soil and they should root easily.

This precious herb has a valued place in the cook's garden, too. It will give a fresh, lemony flavour to summer drinks and fruit salad, tea and hot winter toddies, cakes, and apricot or peach jam.

Lemon balm

Cooking
with mint

I would go so far as to say that most food is enhanced by mint. Perhaps its most traditional companions are peas and new potatoes, and old favourites are mint sauce and minted fruit drinks. But over the years I have experimented a great deal with all the varieties of mint in many different combinations and now, years later, I can offer my favourite recipes to you with confidence. I am sure that after trying them you will agree that mint goes with just about everything!

EQUIVALENT MEASUREMENTS

1 teaspoon = 5 ml
1 tablespoon = 15 ml
1 cup = 250 ml

Soups

Mint complements vegetable soups particularly well, especially green vegetables such as peas, celery, courgettes, lettuce and cucumber. In summer a cold soup made with vegetables and fresh mint is a gloriously refreshing way to begin a meal.

MINT AND LENTIL SOUP
Serves 6

Delicious served hot or cold, this is an excellent standby soup and it keeps well in the fridge.

2 tablespoons olive oil
2 small onions, finely chopped
3 cups uncooked lentils
2 small carrots, grated
2 small potatoes, grated
2 sticks celery, finely chopped
1 tablespoon vinegar
6 cups good stock
2 teaspoons sea salt
cayenne pepper to taste
2 tablespoons apple mint or garden mint, chopped

Lightly brown the onions in the oil. Add all the other ingredients and simmer gently with the lid on until the lentils are tender (about 30 minutes). Give it a stir every now and then. Serve with a sprinkling of fresh mint.

GARDEN PEA AND MINT SOUP
Serves 6–8

This has to be everyone's favourite and it's very quick to make.

little oil
2 onions, finely chopped
1 large potato, peeled and finely grated
1 kg fresh shelled green peas
2 litres good chicken stock
1 large apple, peeled and finely grated
4 teaspoons brown sugar
3 sprigs fresh garden mint
sea salt and black pepper to taste

Lightly brown the onions and potatoes in the oil. Add all the other ingredients. Simmer with the lid on for 10–15 minutes. Pour everything into a liquidiser and blend until smooth. Serve hot in bowls with a dash of cream in the centre, dust with coarsely ground black pepper and add a sprinkling of chopped fresh mint.

Green soup
Serves 6–8

A meal in itself, this is a family favourite.

1 onion, finely chopped
1 cup celery stalks and leaves, finely chopped
3 cups courgettes, thinly sliced
4 cups spinach, thinly shredded and chopped
1 cup split peas
¼ cup fresh parsley, chopped
¼ cup fresh garden or Bowles mint, chopped
6 cups good stock
freshly squeezed juice of 1 lemon
sea salt and cayenne pepper to taste

Sauté the onions and celery until soft. Add all the other ingredients and simmer for 15 minutes. Pour into a liquidiser, blend until smooth, then pour back into the pot to reheat. Add a dash of Worcester sauce. Adjust seasonings. Serve piping hot with croutons, sprinkled with a little chopped mint.

CHILLED CUCUMBER SOUP

Serves 6

Cool, refreshing, quick and easy, this is excellent for summer. For variation add a pinch of curry powder, finely chopped garlic or a touch of Tabasco sauce.

2 large cucumbers, washed then finely grated
1 large onion, finely chopped
4 cups plain yoghurt
2 cups stock
½ cup apple mint or garden mint, finely chopped
sea salt and cayenne pepper to taste

Put everything into the liquidiser and liquidise for 3 minutes or until fully blended. Serve in glass bowls with a sprinkling of mint and sesame seeds. With garlic bread or rolls and some goat's milk cheese and olives, it becomes a feast!

Fish dishes

The nicest mints to use with fish are lemon balm, garden mint or apple mint. The mint enhances the flavour of the fish and makes it beautifully digestible. Chopped mint in lemon juice served over any seafood, particularly calamari, is glorious.

BUTTERED HAKE FILLETS WITH MINT
Serves 4–6

I always keep a box of hake fillets in the freezer for a quick supper dish. This is a delicious way to prepare them.

4–6 hake fillets, rolled in beaten egg and then flour
about 4 tablespoons butter
2 tablespoons fresh chopped mint
1 tablespoon fresh chopped parsley
sea salt and pepper
fresh lemon wedges

In a wide frying pan quickly fry the fish in the butter, turning it to cook on both sides. Drain on a crumpled paper towel. Season and sprinkle with the mixed chopped mint and parsley. Serve hot with new peas and mashed potatoes, with lemon wedges.

GRANDMOTHER'S PICKLED FISH
Serves 6–8

This is my grandmother's recipe and is without a doubt the best pickled fish I've ever tasted. It must be refrigerated for at least two days before being eaten and keeps well in the fridge.

2½ kg Cape salmon or kingklip, or any firm fish
5 onions, thinly sliced in rings
2 green apples, peeled, cored and sliced
3 cups grape vinegar
1 cup water
1½ cups sugar
1 tablespoon turmeric
1–2 tablespoons curry powder (according to taste)
2 teaspoons crushed coriander seeds
1 tablespoon grated fresh ginger
3 fresh bay leaves
2 tablespoons fresh garden mint, chopped
4 teaspoons sea salt

Clean and fillet the fish and cut it into neat pieces. Mix all the other ingredients together and simmer in a heavy-bottomed saucepan for 15 minutes. Add the fish pieces and simmer for a further 20 minutes. Carefully lift the fish out and arrange it neatly in a serving dish. Pour the sauce over it. Cover and cool, and refrigerate for at least 2 days before serving.

This is excellent with beetroot or cabbage salad and makes a superb starter too, served on a lettuce leaf, sprinkled with fresh chopped mint and served with a bread stick.

SUMMER FISH SALAD WITH MINT
Serves 4–6

This quick and easy salad is excellent as a starter, a summer luncheon dish, a sandwich filling or for a picnic, served with fresh bread rolls, olives and a potato salad.

6 hake or cod fillets (or any filleted fish)
1 onion, sliced
2 fresh bay leaves
1 cup mayonnaise
2 tablespoons finely chopped onion
1 cup celery, thinly sliced
1 green apple, peeled, cored and diced
1 cup cucumber, peeled and chopped
1 teaspoon sea salt
cayenne pepper
lettuce leaves
2 hard-boiled eggs, finely chopped
juice of 1 lemon
1 tablespoon fresh mint, finely chopped

Poach the skinned fillets of fish in a little water with the onion, bay leaves and a little salt until tender. Then drain and flake the fish. Leave to cool. Mix the mayonnaise with the chopped onion, celery, apple and cucumber. Add salt and cayenne pepper and fold in the flaked fish. Spoon onto lettuce leaves in individual glass dishes and sprinkle with the hard-boiled egg, lemon juice and chopped mint. Serve chilled with a wedge of lemon and a dash of cayenne pepper.

MINTY FISH BAKE
Serves 6

This can be baked in the oven or over a braai. Vary the vegetables if you wish with sliced potatoes, mushrooms, aubergines or fresh mealies cut off the cob.

2 tablespoons olive oil
6 pieces cod, hake or kingklip, skinned and deboned
salt and freshly ground black pepper to taste
2 tablespoons fresh garden mint, chopped
juice of 1 or 2 lemons
2 tomatoes, sliced
2 green peppers, sliced

Cut off 6 squares of tin foil, each about 30 cm square. Liberally wipe them with the oil. Place one piece of fish in the middle of each square, sprinkle with salt, pepper, chopped mint and lemon juice. Top with the tomato and green pepper slices (or a variation), drizzle with more oil and lemon juice, salt and pepper. Fold the foil to form a parcel.

Place the foil parcels on a baking tray or in hot coals. Bake at 180 °C for 20–30 minutes or until the fish is cooked through. Turn out onto hot plates and serve with fresh chopped mint and lemon wedges.

> ❧ HANDY HINT
> Sprinkle fresh, finely chopped lemon balm or spearmint leaves into a bowl of mayonnaise and serve as a delicious accompaniment to fish.

Meat dishes

Through the centuries mint has been a popular culinary companion for all types of meat, tenderising tough meats and imparting a light and refreshing flavour.

ROAST LAMB WITH MINT SAUCE
Serves 6–8

This is a classic dish, suitable for any occasion. Serve with any vegetables, such as peas, gem squash and rice, and traditional mint sauce (see page 50).

leg or shoulder of lamb
sea salt and pepper to taste
½ cup fresh garden mint, chopped
juice of 1 lemon
6–8 potatoes, peeled and halved
3 onions, peeled and halved
little sunflower cooking oil
2 cups water

Place the lamb in a large baking dish or iron pot. Sprinkle with salt and pepper and rub in well on all sides. Sprinkle with the chopped mint and lemon juice. Tuck the potatoes and onions in around the meat and dribble a little sunflower oil over everything. Add the water. Replace the lid. Bake at 180 °C for 2–3 hours or until the lamb is browned and succulent and tender. Check it at intervals and add more water if necessary.

BEEF OLIVES
Serves 4–6

This dish is an excellent party piece and so easy to make. The stuffing can be varied according to taste, but this one is my favourite. Ask the butcher to thinly slice the rump steak.

6 very thin slices rump steak

Stuffing
3 tablespoons sunflower cooking oil
3 tablespoons onion, finely chopped
2 cloves garlic, finely chopped (optional)
½ cup green pepper, finely chopped
1½ cups fresh wholewheat breadcrumbs
½ cup mint, finely chopped (garden mint or apple mint)
½ cup celery, finely chopped
sea salt and cayenne pepper to taste
juice of 1 lemon
about 1 cup good beef stock
½ cup red wine

Place the steak slices between sheets of waxed paper and beat with a mallet to an even thinness. Trim.

Fry the onions, garlic and celery in the oil until golden. Add the green pepper and fry, then add the breadcrumbs. Add all the ingredients except the stock and the wine. Stir briskly all the time to form a stiff dough. Divide the filling between the slices of beef, spreading it evenly over, then roll up the pieces and tie them neatly with string. Fry these in a little oil until evenly browned.

Place the beef olives in a casserole dish, pour over the stock and the wine and add 2–4 mint sprigs. Cover and bake for 1 hour or until tender, basting occasionally. Serve on a bed of mashed potatoes with the gravy from the baking spooned over it. Garnish with sprigs of mint. Served with garden peas and a salad, this is a superb meal.

Minted pork chops
Serves 4–6

For variation add thickly sliced potatoes, sweet potatoes or halved mushrooms.

6–8 lean pork chops, thinly sliced and trimmed of excess fat
3 tablespoons honey
freshly ground black pepper
sea salt to taste
4 tablespoons fresh garden mint, chopped
2 teaspoons crushed allspice berries
juice of 1 lemon

Lay the chops in a baking dish. Mix all the other ingredients well and spread evenly over the chops. Cover the dish and bake at 180 °C for approximately 30–40 minutes or until the chops are browned and tender. Baste the chops every now and then with the honey and mint mixture and turn them over halfway through the cooking time to ensure that they are evenly browned.

> **❧ Handy Hint**
> Serve chopped fresh spearmint with rich meat dishes to aid digestion.

Poultry dishes

The fresh taste of mint is superb with poultry, particularly in stuffing, marinades and stir fries. Sprinkle it fresh over grilled chicken, cold chicken sandwiches and chicken salad. Garden mint, apple mint, corn mint and the spearmints are best with poultry.

TURKEY STIR FRY WITH MINT
Serves 4–6

This tasty supper dish is made in just a few minutes, which makes it the ideal recipe after the slog of Christmas dinner, and it uses up the turkey, which tends to be a bit dry when it's cold.

little oil
2 onions, finely chopped
about 4 cups cold, cooked turkey, neatly cubed
3–4 cups (500 g) mushrooms, thinly sliced OR
1 tin asparagus pieces, drained
½ cup chopped pecan nuts
sea salt and cayenne pepper to taste
juice of 1 lemon
2 tablespoons fresh garden mint, finely chopped

Brown the onion lightly in the oil. Add the cubes of turkey and lightly stir fry, turning constantly until heated through. Add all the other ingredients except for the mint. Keep everything moving until the mushrooms are tender, then sprinkle with mint and more lemon juice. Serve immediately, with rice.

BAKED MINTED CHICKEN WITH VEGETABLES
Serves 4–6

Substitute duck or turkey here if you prefer.

1 chicken braai pack (about 8 chicken pieces)
2 onions, chopped
4 leeks, thinly sliced
4 carrots, peeled and thinly sliced
4–6 potatoes, peeled and quartered
4–6 whole tomatoes, skinned
sea salt and freshly ground black pepper to taste
juice of 1 lemon
little sunflower cooking oil
½–1 litre good chicken stock
½ cup apple mint, finely chopped

Lay the chicken pieces in a large baking tray or flat casserole dish. Sprinkle the onion, leeks and carrots all around. Place the potatoes and tomatoes between the chicken pieces. Sprinkle with salt, pepper, lemon juice and a little oil. Add half the chicken stock. Cover with tin foil and place on the middle shelf of the oven. Roast at 180 °C for 1–1½ hours or until the chicken is golden and crisp. Add a little more stock from time to time to prevent the vegetables from burning and take care not to break the tomatoes.

Remove from the oven and sprinkle with the mint. Serve immediately with a green salad and bread rolls to mop up the delicious gravy.

CHICKEN LIVER GRILL
Serves 4–6

This is a stunning starter to serve at a party. The freshness of the mint is superb here as it counteracts the richness of the chicken livers.

1 carton chicken livers
little oil
1 onion, finely chopped
1 tablespoon fresh grated ginger
little sea salt and freshly ground black pepper
6–10 rindless bacon rashers, chopped
juice of 1 lemon
few drops Tabasco sauce
6–10 large brown mushrooms
½ cup fresh garden mint, chopped

Quickly fry the chicken livers in the oil with the onion, ginger, sea salt and black pepper. Lift out of the pan and put aside. In the same pan fry the bacon until crisp. Drain on absorbent paper. Mix the bacon and the chicken livers. Mash with the lemon juice and the Tabasco sauce.

Use a sharp pointed knife to remove the stalks of the mushrooms and place them underside up on a baking sheet. Spoon neat rounds of the chicken liver mixture into the little hollow of each mushroom. Place under the grill for 2–4 minutes — just long enough to soften the mushrooms slightly.

Sprinkle with the mint and serve hot on small, warmed plates with wedges of lemon.

Vegetables

Fresh, finely chopped mint transforms the most ordinary vegetables. Peas, dried beans, lentils, barley, pumpkin, squash, sweet potatoes and aubergines are excellent companions, to name but a few. You can use not only garden mint or apple mint, but spearmint or corn mint too.

STUFFED PEPPERS
Serves 6

6 large green peppers
little sunflower cooking oil
4 tablespoons onion, finely
　chopped
1 cup cooked rice
1 cup grated cheddar cheese
2 eggs, well beaten
1 teaspoon sea salt

cayenne pepper to taste
2 teaspoons Worcester sauce
2 teaspoons fresh parsley, chopped
2 tablespoons fresh garden mint,
　chopped
2 tablespoons butter
1 litre chicken stock

Slice the tops off the peppers at the stem end and scoop out the pulp and seeds. Brown the onion in the oil. Stir in the rice, cheese, eggs, seasoning and herbs. Mix until well blended and thick. Stuff the peppers with this mixture.

Stand the peppers up in a deep baking dish so that they don't fall over. Dot with butter and pour in the stock. Replace the top of each pepper to form a lid and bake for about 30 minutes at 180 °C. Baste the peppers with the stock every now and then. Serve hot on a bed of mashed potato, with a green salad.

STUFFED MARROW

Serves 4
This is one of my favourite dishes in midsummer when marrows are abundant.

little oil
1 onion, chopped
2 tablespoons celery, chopped
2 cups lean mince
salt and cayenne pepper to taste
juice of 1 lemon
1 cup water or stock

2 tablespoons tomato sauce
1 medium marrow
2 tablespoons mint, chopped
1 beaten egg
grated cheddar cheese
butter
sprig of mint

Sauté the onion, celery and mince in the oil. Add the salt, pepper and lemon juice. Add water or stock and tomato sauce. Simmer gently until done and allow to cool. Cut the end off the marrow and peel the skin with a potato peeler. Hollow out the seeds and discard. Mix the mint and the beaten egg into the mince mixture, and spoon into the marrow. With toothpicks secure the sliced-off end of the marrow over the opening to seal it.

Place the stuffed marrow in a large casserole dish, sprinkle with grated cheese and dot with butter. Add 1 cup water and tuck in a sprig of mint under the marrow. Cover and bake for 30–40 minutes at 180 °C or until the marrow is tender. Sprinkle with more freshly chopped garden mint and serve hot with rice and a green salad.

AUBERGINE AND MINT STIR FRY
Serves 4–6

In Spain and Portugal this tasty supper dish is often served with a cup of plain yoghurt and chillies as a side dish for curries. Alternatively, add 2 cups chopped mushrooms and serve it on a bed of rice.

sunflower cooking oil
1 large aubergine, peeled and thinly sliced
2 large onions, finely chopped
3 green peppers, seeded and finely chopped
2 apples, peeled and diced
1–2 teaspoons chopped garlic (optional)
2 tablespoons fresh garden mint, chopped
sea salt and cayenne pepper to taste
1 teaspoon ground nutmeg
juice of 1 lemon
2 teaspoons honey

Cover the aubergines with salted water and soak for 30 minutes. In a wok or large frying pan, stir fry the onions and aubergines until golden. Add all the other ingredients and stir fry until tender. Add a little water if necessary to prevent drying out.

Serve piping hot on baked potatoes that have been cut open and sprinkled with fresh, chopped garden mint.

Mint tabbouleh

Serves 6–8

There are many variations of this nutritious Middle Eastern salad, all tasting strongly of mint. I was taught how to make it by an Israeli who had lived with the Bedouin for several years and this is exactly as they made it there under the desert palms.

2 cups cracked wheat, soaked overnight
sea salt and cayenne pepper to taste
⅔ cup honey
⅔ cup brown grape vinegar
1 cup celery stalks, finely chopped
1 green pepper, finely chopped
1 red pepper, finely chopped
1 cup fresh garden mint, finely chopped

Soak the cracked wheat overnight in cold water with a sprig of garden mint.

Mix the salt, pepper, honey and vinegar by placing them together in a screw-top jar and shaking well. Drain the wheat well. If the grains are not tender enough, cook them up with fresh water, fresh mint and a teaspoon of sea salt for a further 10–20 minutes. Drain and cool.

Mix all the other ingredients, add the honey and vinegar mixture and stir well. Serve in a big salad bowl decorated with mint and olives.

Desserts

Spearmint, peppermint, chocolate mint and lemon balm best complement desserts. Chocolate mint in particular is glorious with chocolate desserts. I have included here some of my personal favourites, but try adding mint to some of your own favourite recipes: you will find the combination quite delicious.

CHOCOLATE MINT ICE-CREAM
Serves 4–6

4 cups thick cream
4 tablespoons chocolate mint leaves, finely chopped
3 eggs, separated and the whites stiffly beaten
1 cup white sugar
1 tablespoon cocoa powder
200 g bitter dark chocolate, finely grated
1 teaspoon vanilla essence

Add the mint to 3 cups of the cream, cover and chill overnight in the fridge.

Beat the egg yolks with the sugar, cocoa, chocolate and vanilla essence. Add 1 cup cream and beat again. Whisk the minted cream that you refrigerated overnight until it thickens, then fold in the egg, sugar and cream mixture. Fold in the stiffly beaten egg whites. Pour the mixture into freezing trays and stir every 20 minutes until frozen.

Serve with finely chopped chocolate mint sprinkled on top and a dusting of cocoa powder.

MINT SORBET
Serves 4–6

This is the perfect after-dinner digestive, particularly after a heavy meal, or it can be served between courses at an elaborate dinner to clear the palate.

2 cups water
1 cup castor sugar
2 tablespoons spearmint or peppermint, finely chopped
juice of 1 lemon
3 egg whites, stiffly beaten

Boil the water and castor sugar for 5 minutes. Remove from the stove and allow to cool for a few minutes. Add the mint, stir and stand covered until completely cool, then strain out the mint and add the lemon juice. Very gently fold in the stiffly beaten egg whites. Pour into a freezing tray and put it into the freezer. Stir or whisk lightly just as it is beginning to set. Freeze again.

Remove from the freezer 5 minutes before serving. Sprinkle with fresh chopped chocolate mint and serve in small glass dishes decorated with a chocolate mint sprig.

Minted apple snow

Serves 4–6

This is a wonderfully light summer dessert.

1 kg green cooking apples, peeled, cored and cubed
juice of 2 oranges
4 tablespoons honey
4 peppermint sprigs (black or green)
1 tablespoon finely grated orange rind
3 eggs, separated and the whites stiffly beaten

Gently stew the apples in the orange juice with the honey and mint until they are soft. Discard the mint and place the apples in a blender. Blend to a smooth pulp. Fold in the stiffly beaten egg whites. Spoon into glass dishes, top with a mint leaf or two and a glacé cherry. Serve chilled.

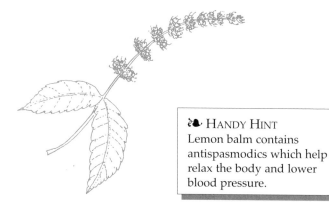

❧ HANDY HINT
Lemon balm contains antispasmodics which help relax the body and lower blood pressure.

CHOCOLATE MINT MOUSSE
Serves 4–6

The combination of chocolate and mint in this mousse is simply sublime.

250 g dark chocolate
2 tablespoons fresh chocolate mint, finely chopped
3 extra large eggs, separated
⅔ cup brown caramel sugar
250 ml thick cream
3 tablespoons soft butter

In a double boiler melt the chocolate with the chocolate mint. Meanwhile beat the egg whites until stiff and in a separate bowl beat the egg yolks with the sugar. Whip the cream until stiff. Remove the melted chocolate from the stove and whisk in the soft butter. Add the beaten egg yolks and sugar. Mix lightly. Add the cream and finally fold in the egg whites, lightly blending everything. Pour into pretty glass dishes. Chill. Just before serving, decorate with a swirl of cream and a sprig of fresh peppermint, or dust with cocoa. As a special treat sprinkle a crushed peppermint crisp over the chocolate mousse.

MINTED WATERMELON
Serves 4–6

Served as a starter or dessert, this is a superb summer cooler. The mint and sugar mixture can be sprinkled directly onto thick watermelon slices or served with spanspek or green melon balls stacked in a tall glass serving dish and decorated with crystallised mint leaves (see page 52). Be sure to dry the mint thoroughly in a towel before chopping it or it will dissolve the sugar.

slices of watermelon or melon balls, arranged prettily in glass dishes
1 cup fresh mint, finely chopped (spearmint or lemon balm)
1½ cups white sugar

Mix the well-dried and chopped mint with the sugar and allow to stand for a minute or two. Meanwhile arrange the watermelon slices or balls prettily in glass dishes. Sprinkle the mint and sugar in between the balls or onto the slices. Serve chilled, decorated with little sprigs of mint or crystallised mint leaves.

Baking with mint

Just about any recipe for muffins, cakes and tarts will taste good with the addition of chopped mint, so you can experiment by adding mint to your favourite recipes. The varieties to use are spearmint, eau de cologne mint, chocolate mint or pineapple mint, all of which taste divine in baking.

GREEN MEALIE AND MINT BREAD
Serves 4–6

2 eggs
pinch sea salt
3 teaspoons honey
2–3 tablespoons milk
6 green mealies, cooked and cut off the cob
½ tablespoon baking powder
1 tablespoon chopped lemon balm

Beat the eggs with the salt, honey and milk. Mix with the mealies and add the baking powder and lemon balm. Spoon into a greased bowl. Tie a double layer of greaseproof paper over the bowl to form a watertight lid and steam in a large pot of water for approximately 2 hours. Slice and spread with mint butter (see page 51).

DATE REFRIGERATOR CAKE
Serves 6–8

This is popular with children for a school lunch box treat. For variation the nuts can be replaced with sunflower or sesame seeds, or both.

250 g butter
¾ cup brown caramel sugar
2 eggs
1 teaspoon vanilla essence
1 cup dates, chopped
½ cup pecan nuts, chopped
1 tablespoon eau de cologne mint, chopped
1 packet plain biscuits, such as Marie or Tennis biscuits
sprigs of lemon balm

Melt the butter with the sugar. Whisk in the eggs and vanilla essence. Add the dates, nuts and mint. Break the biscuits into small pieces without crumbling them and stir them into the mixture. Line a flat baking dish with baking paper and oil lightly. Press in the mixture evenly and place in the fridge to set. Cut into small squares once it has set. Serve on a cake plate decorated with sprigs of lemon balm.

LEMON AND COCONUT TART
Serves 6–8

This divinely rich, sweet tart is best served in small portions, with mint or lemon balm tea — iced or hot.

Crust
1 egg
1½ tablespoons sugar
3 tablespoons soft butter

1 cup cake flour
1 teaspoon baking powder
little water

Whisk the egg and the sugar. Add the soft butter and mix gently. Fold in the flour and the baking powder and work into a dough with the water. Press into an ovenproof flan dish.

Topping
1 egg
½ cup sugar
½ cup soft butter

1 teaspoon vanilla essence
2 cups desiccated coconut

Beat the egg, sugar, butter and vanilla essence together. Add the coconut. Roll into a ball. Wrap in greaseproof paper and chill.

Filling
2 eggs
2 tins condensed milk
¾ cup fresh lemon juice

2 tablespoons lemon balm or
   peppermint, finely chopped

Beat the eggs. Mix the condensed milk with the lemon juice and add to the beaten eggs. Add the mint and stir well.

To assemble the tart, pour the filling into the crust. On the coarsest side of the grater, grate the coconut topping (it should resemble large crumbs), evenly covering the condensed milk mixture. Bake at 180 °C for 20–25 minutes until it is lightly brown.

Drinks

Mint's marvellous digestive properties and ability to quell nausea combined with its refreshing taste have made it a popular addition to drinks for many centuries.

MINT JULEP
Serves 1

4 teaspoons sugar
4 teaspoons water
crushed ice

25 ml whisky
4–6 spearmint or peppermint leaves
sprig of mint

Mix the sugar into the water and stir until dissolved. Place a little crushed ice in a glass. Add the syrup, whisky and spearmint or peppermint leaves. Stir well, crushing the mint. Top with crushed ice and more whisky if you wish. Decorate with a sprig of mint and serve when the glass starts to frost.

MINT SYRUP
Makes about 1 litre

2 cups fresh corn mint or
   spearmint, chopped
juice of 3 lemons
3 cups sugar

2 teaspoons lemon zest
1 stick cinnamon
10 cloves
1 litre water

Boil up everything together for 5–7 minutes. Leave to cool, then strain. Serve diluted with iced water or fruit juice.

MINT AFTER-DINNER TEA
Makes 1 cup

This should become part of every menu, it is such an excellent digestive.

¼ cup fresh mint leaves (peppermint, spearmint or lemon balm are
  excellent here)
1 cup boiling water

Pour the boiling water over the mint leaves. Stand for 5 minutes, then strain.

DRIED MINT TEA BLEND
In a pretty screw-top jar this dried mint blend makes a beautiful and thoughtful gift.

1 cup dried peppermint leaves
1 cup dried lemon balm leaves
1 cup dried eau de cologne mint leaves
1 cup dried rose petals
6 sticks cinnamon, roughly crumbled

To dry the mint leaves, place sprigs of mint on sheets of newspaper in the shade and turn them daily until they are dry. Strip the leaves off the stalks. Mix everything together and store in a screw-top jar.

Use 1 tablespoon of the dried mixture per cup of tea. Pour over boiling water and allow to steep for about 8–10 minutes. Strain. Drinking it unsweetened is best.

PEPPERMINT LIQUEUR
Makes 1 bottle

Served in tiny liqueur glasses or over cracked ice, this home-made liqueur makes a dinner party unforgettable. It is also a stunning gift for the person who has everything.

2 tablespoons peppermint, chopped
1 tablespoon lemon balm, chopped
1 cinnamon stick
1 whole nutmeg, crushed
10 cloves
1 cup sugar
rind of 1 lemon, finely pared
½ bottle good brandy

Mix everything together. Pour into a jar with a well-fitting lid and store in a dark place for at least 1 month. Shake up daily. Strain and decant into a pretty bottle and store in a dark cupboard to mature further. It is at its most delicious after 2 months — if you can wait that long!

> **HANDY HINT**
> For a delicious cup of coffee, add 3 or 4 Cape velvet mint leaves to a cup of hot black coffee, bruising the leaves with a spoon. Sip slowly without milk or sugar.

SEKANJABIN
Makes about 1½ litres

This refreshing and reviving drink originated in Persia, and perhaps remains rather unusual in the Western world. It must be served very cold.

4 cups water
3 cups white sugar
few parings of lemon rind
2 tablespoons fresh spearmint, corn mint or peppermint, finely chopped
2 cups good white wine
2 tablespoons brown grape vinegar
3 tablespoons cucumber, peeled and finely grated

Boil the water and sugar until the sugar dissolves. Mix in the lemon rind and mint and cool. Mix in all the remaining ingredients. Chill well and serve over cracked ice or with a little iced water.

For the gourmet

These are all old favourites, particularly the mint jelly and mint sauce. I was taught how to make both of these by my grandmother and I feel it is a shame to limit them to lamb: they are excellent accompaniments to so many savoury dishes. Try them with chicken and pasta, on cucumber sandwiches, baked potatoes and pumpkin, over steaming carrots and chilled beetroot salad, potato salad and hot and cold bean dishes.

CLASSIC MINT SAUCE
Makes a small jar

½ cup garden mint, finely chopped
½ cup sugar
½ cup brown grape vinegar
½ cup warm water

Place all the ingredients in a screw-top jar and shake until the sugar has dissolved. Pour into a jug for serving. This sauce keeps well in the fridge in a sealed jar.

MINT JELLY
Makes 2–3 small jars

This classic is particularly good with mutton, pork, poultry and pasta dishes.

3 tablespoons gelatine
1 cup fresh garden mint, finely chopped
1 cup white sugar
2 cups warm water
1 cup fresh lemon juice or white grape vinegar

Dissolve the gelatine in a little warm water. Mix all the other ingredients, stirring well to dissolve the sugar. Stir in the gelatine mixture briskly. Pour into small jars with tight lids. Refrigerate for at least 3 hours before using.

MINT BUTTER
Serves 6

I provide tiny individual butter dishes with mint butter for each guest at dinner parties, to use with everything from melba toast and bread rolls to steamed cauliflower and green peas.

1 cup soft butter
½ cup garden mint or apple mint, finely chopped

Mash the mint into the butter and mix well. Use on steamed vegetables, pasta dishes, bread sticks or melba toast, or as a spread on sandwiches with lettuce and cucumber.

CRYSTALLISED MINT LEAVES

These are stunning decorations for cakes and desserts. The mint leaves must be absolutely dry before you begin the process of crystallisation.

fresh mint leaves, well dried (spearmint is the nicest)
3 egg whites
1 cup castor sugar

Beat the egg whites well, but not too stiffly. Dip each mint leaf first into the beaten egg whites and then into the castor sugar, taking care that each side is well coated. Place on greaseproof paper and dry in a draught, for example in front of a window, but out of sunlight. Store in an airtight tin.

CHOCOLATE MINT LEAVES

mint leaves (chocolate mint or Cape velvet mint)
1 slab dark chocolate

Melt the chocolate in a double boiler. Dip each mint leaf into the chocolate, coating both sides. Dry on greaseproof paper until firm, keeping them out of sunlight, or place in the fridge to harden on a hot day. Serve on cakes or ice cream.

Mint in cosmetics

In ancient times the Greeks, Romans and Egyptians used mint in their bath houses to freshen and cleanse the water. They are known to have taken the herb with them on their voyages of discovery to both clean their teeth and wash with. It would have been stored dry, and then soaked in water to revive it before using.

Records have been found indicating that mint was used centuries ago to clear the skin of spots, acne, rashes and itches, and to treat varicose veins and chilblains.

Today mint is a desirable and important ingredient in skin preparations such as creams, oils and shampoos. It has the marvellous ability to dissolve oily deposits on the skin and hair, and can be easily utilised in homemade preparations.

MINT AND APPLE CIDER VINEGAR RINSE
Makes 1 bottle

This versatile rinse can be massaged into the scalp before washing the hair, or a dash added to the rinsing water after washing the face. Dab onto the skin to clear up spots, pimples and to counteract oily skin. Add ½ cup to the bath to heal rashes, spots and skin ailments in general. It helps to adjust the acid balance of the skin and will soothe dry, itchy, flaky skin.

6–8 sprigs spearmint, peppermint or lemon balm
1 bottle apple cider vinegar

Push the mint into the bottle of vinegar. Stand in the sun for 10 days, during which time strain and discard the spent sprigs twice and replace with fresh ones of the same variety. Finally, strain the vinegar and discard the old sprigs. Pour into a clean bottle, and add a fresh sprig for identification.

MINT CLEANSING AND HEALING CREAM
Makes 1 jar

I use this rather old-fashioned cream frequently for rough skin on the feet and to ease aches, cramps and muscle spasm in my legs and neck. It is wonderful during the hot summer months for deep cleansing the skin on the face and neck.

Should you want to preserve it and use it as a massage cream, add 2 teaspoons wheatgerm oil after straining.

1 cup aqueous cream
1 cup mixed fresh chopped peppermint, eau de cologne mint
*   and lemon balm*

Warm the ingredients together gently in a double boiler for 20 minutes. Leave to stand for 10 minutes, then strain and pour into a sterilised jar.

MINT LIP BALM
This is a wonderful healing balm for chapped lips.

2 teaspoons white beeswax
8 teaspoons cocoa butter
2 teaspoons lanolin
½ teaspoon wheatgerm oil
2 tablespoons chopped fresh peppermint, lemon balm,
*   eau de cologne mint, or a combination*

In a double boiler warm all the ingredients for 15 minutes. Strain immediately and pour into a small, flat tin or jar. Apply frequently.

DEODORISING FOOT POWDER

Use this refreshing powder to dust the feet and sprinkle in the shoes, especially in summer.

½ cup dried peppermint, finely sieved
1 cup cornflour
1 teaspoon pure essential peppermint oil
2 teaspoons powdered cloves

Mix everything very well. Keep in a sealed jar.

MINT SCRUB

This is a marvellous cleanser for spotty, greasy skin, but also a superb exfoliator and refresher for dry skin, especially after the cold and dryness of winter. Many beauty schools use it for teenage skins, as well as a cleanser for pollutants on all skin types.

1 cup boiling water
½ cup peppermint leaves, chopped
1 cup oats
1 teaspoon almond oil
1½ tablespoons honey

Pour the boiling water over the peppermint leaves. Stand until lukewarm, then soak the oats in the lukewarm extract. Work well together by mixing and pressing. Add the almond oil and honey and mash well. Apply to the face and neck, and lie back and relax for 10 minutes. Rinse off with mint and apple cider vinegar rinse (page 54). Pat dry and enjoy the glorious freshness!

Any left over scrub is excellent for calloused feet.

Medicinal uses of mint

Remember: *Always consult your doctor before starting any home treatment.*

Since ancient times peppermint has been regarded as an excellent digestive, soothing nausea, heartburn, flatulence and vomiting. It is invaluable in treating chilblains, haemorrhoids, varicose veins and all circulatory disorders. It stimulates the gall bladder and the liver, and eases stress and tension, including premenstrual tension.

Menthol is an active ingredient in mint which helps to clear the sinuses and congestion in the head and chest.

STANDARD MINT BREW
Makes 1 cup

To treat *indigestion, acne, arthritis, nervousness, rheumatism, headaches, colds and coughs, cramps, nervous and premenstrual tension, and circulatory disorders* such as *haemorrhoids, varicose veins and chilblains*, take 1 cup of this standard mint brew per day for about 10 days. Break for 1 week, then continue every day or on alternate days for another 10 days.

½ cup fresh mint leaves (peppermint, spearmint or corn mint are nicest)
1 cup boiling water

Pour the boiling water over the mint leaves. Stand for 5 minutes, strain and sip slowly.

MINT OINTMENT
As an ointment for *chilblains, varicose veins and haemorrhoids*, this simple cream is soothing and gentle.

1 cup fresh mint leaves, roughly chopped (spearmint or peppermint are wonderful here)
1 cup aqueous cream
2 teaspoons witch hazel
1 teaspoon wheatgerm oil

Warm the mint and aqueous cream in a double boiler for 15 minutes. Stir every now and then, strain and add the witch hazel and wheatgerm oil. Stir well. Pour into a sterilised jar and apply lavishly to the afflicted area.

Mint lotion

Use this is a soothing wash or dab on skin for *sunburn, rashes, light grazes and insect bites and stings*. Make it fresh often and use it liberally.

2 cups fresh spearmint or peppermint leaves
1 cup yarrow leaves
1 litre boiling water

Boil everything together for 10 minutes with the lid on. Cool, keeping covered until pleasantly warm. Strain and dab on or wash over the affected area.

Mint tea for colds and flu

Sip a cup of this tea as required.

1 cup fresh mint leaves (any variety)
½ cup fresh sage leaves
1 stick cinnamon
2 litres water

Boil up all the ingredients for 10 minutes with the lid on. Stand aside to cool until pleasantly warm. Strain. Sip a little at a time. Store the rest in the refrigerator, taking out a cup at a time to warm up as required.

> ❧ HANDY HINT
> Rub mint leaves on an insect bite to stop it from itching.

MINT TEA FOR NAUSEA AND FEVER

This drink is also excellent for *cramps, including menstrual cramps, bloating, colic and severe indigestion.* Made with lemon balm, it is wonderful for pregnant women.

1 cup fresh mint (peppermint is best here)
1 tablespoon freshly sliced or grated ginger root
2 cups boiling water
juice of ½ lemon

Pour the boiling water over the mint and ginger. Stand for 5 minutes, then strain. Add the lemon juice. Sip slowly while hot, a little at a time. Even just wetting the lips and tongue will help to allay that awful nauseous feeling.

MINT TEA FOR DIGESTIVE UPSETS

With the addition of ½ cup yarrow leaves, this tea can also be taken internally or used as a rinse to clear up *acne*.

½ cup fresh spearmint or peppermint sprigs
2 cups boiling water
3 cloves
dash apple cider vinegar (optional)

Simmer everything except the vinegar together for 5 minutes. Add the apple cider vinegar if desired. Stir well. Drink ½ cup daily, taken a tablespoonful at a time.

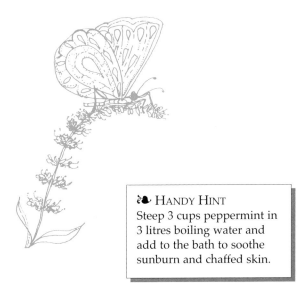

> **✦ HANDY HINT**
> Steep 3 cups peppermint in 3 litres boiling water and add to the bath to soothe sunburn and chaffed skin.

Mint compress

This soothing compress will relieve the *itchiness of bites and rashes*.

1 cup boiling water
1 cup corn mint or chocolate mint leaves

Pour the boiling water over the mint leaves. Stand and cool until pleasantly warm, then lay the softened, warmed sprigs over the affected area. Hold in place with a bandage. Relax for 15 minutes. Remove the compress and dab area with mint lotion (see page 59).

Mint oil

This is a marvellous remedy for *headaches, neuralgia, stiff muscles and tired feet*.

1 cup almond oil
1 cup fresh peppermint and pineapple mint sprigs
10 cloves

Warm everything in a double boiler for 20 minutes. Cool, strain and bottle in a sterilised bottle. Use lavishly as a massage oil, or add a teaspoonful to the bath for aches and pains.

❧ Handy Hint
Drink fresh peppermint tea before an exam to stimulate the memory.

Mint pesticides

The fresh fragrance of mint and its high menthol levels make it an ideal insect repellent and all varieties can be used to make homemade room fresheners, burned outdoors on the braai fire to keep mosquitoes away, added to pot pourris and rubbed onto furniture and even blankets and pillows to keep insects at bay. Pennyroyal in particular is excellent as a mosquito repellent.

When entertaining outdoors in summer place big bowls of pennyroyal near visitors' chairs and encourage them to rub it onto their palms and then onto their legs and arms to keep mosquitoes away. (Caution: do not rub pennyroyal or Corsican mint directly onto the legs and arms as a rash may develop on sensitive skins.)

Pennyroyal insect-repelling candles

Pennyroyal candles are perhaps my most successful insect repellent. On hot summer evenings when mosquitoes are everywhere I burn them on the patio and even indoors.

A quick method is to place several drops of peppermint essential oil around the wick of a large unscented candle. When the wick is lit, the oil burns with it, filling the air with the strong, fresh fragrance.

Better still, make your own mint insect-repelling candles. The peppermint oil is bought at the chemist.

6 plain white candles
½ –1 cup pennyroyal or Corsican mint leaves,
  stripped of their stems
4 teaspoons peppermint oil

To prepare the moulds, use 2 or 3 small, clean ceramic flower pots. Take a plaited piece of string (or plait the wicks from the melted candles together), tie a knot in one end — to block the hole in the flower pot — and tie the other end to a pencil or small stick that rests across the rim of the pot so that the wick hangs in a vertical position.

Melt the candles in an old saucepan on the stove. Add the mint leaves, stirring them in well so that they are evenly distributed. Add 3 teaspoons peppermint oil and stir gently. Immediately pour the melted, scented wax into the prepared moulds. Allow to cool. Save a little wax and reheat it to fill the 'basin' that will form around the wick. Just before it sets, drop in another teaspoon of peppermint oil.

Allow to harden and cure for at least 3 days before lighting.

MINT POT POURRI

I love this pot pourri! It banishes stale cigarette smoke, and cooking and pet smells from a room. Placed in cupboards, it clears mustiness and is particularly useful at the coast when closed rooms and cupboards seem to retain that awful dank smell. In addition it is a wonderful insect-repellent for moths and fishmoths.

1 cup dried minced lemon peel
1 cup mixed cloves and cinnamon pieces
½ cup coriander seeds
½ cup allspice berries
3 cups dried mint leaves (spearmint and eau de cologne mint are best)
3 teaspoons each peppermint and lavender oil

Mix the peel and spices together and pour into a large screw-top jar. Add the peppermint and lavender oil. Shake up well. Leave for 1 week, shaking up daily. Add more oil at the end of the week if you wish.

Meanwhile dry a selection of mints on newspaper in the shade, turning them daily. When they are dry, strip the leaves off the stalks and add them to the peel and spices. Add more oil if you wish and leave for a further week, well corked to enable the oils to penetrate.

Fill little bags or bowls with the pot pourri and place in cupboards or in large open bowls in the room (cover at night). Revive from time to time with more oil: put everything into a screw-top jar or tin, add the oil and shake up. Stand for 2–3 days to allow the oil to penetrate.

MINT INSECT-REPELLING LOTION

This lotion is quick and easy to make and can also be used as a spray, in a bottle with a spritz hand pump or a plant mister (available from nurseries). Rub the lotion onto arms and legs. (If you have sensitive skin, test a little on the inside of your wrist first to check that you are not allergic to it.)

½ cup methylated spirits
1 cup apple cider vinegar
2 teaspoons peppermint essential oil (aromatherapy oil)
1 teaspoon lavender essential oil
½ cup almond oil

Put everything into a screw-top jar and shake up well for at least 5 minutes. Smooth onto arms and legs or spray all around the room. Shake before use.

Rat and mouse repellent

Bunches of mint and lavender keep rats and mice out of the house. Tied with khakibos it even keeps bats away!

bunches of mint and lavender (eau de cologne mint or
*   pineapple mint are best)*
lavender oil
peppermint oil

Tie bunches of mint and lavender together and drop lavender and peppermint oil into the heart of each bunch. Tuck behind doors and in cupboards, especially in autumn when rats and mice seem to be planning their winter nests and hibernation time indoors! Replace with fresh bunches every 10 days or so.

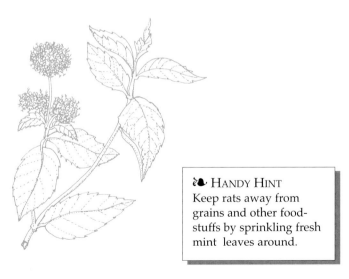

&. Handy Hint
Keep rats away from grains and other food-stuffs by sprinkling fresh mint leaves around.

INDEX